The Dictionary
of Vampspeak

Terminology & Lingo in
the Vampire Community

Second Edition

Sanguinarius

A publication of Sanguinarius.Org

Second Edition

Formerly titled *The Dictionary of Sanguinese.*

ISBN: 1-4499-9506-3
EAN-13: 978-1-4499-9506-5

Published by:
Sanguinarius.org for Real Vampires, Blood Drinkers & Vampiric People
http://www.sanguinarius.org/
publications@sanguinarius.org

Additional copies of this work may be obtained from the following url:
https://www.createspace.com/Customer/EStore.do?id=3421484

This book is for all members of the vampiric community

Introduction

The Dictionary of Vampspeak (formerly titled *The Dictionary of Sanguinese*) is a lexicon of the terminology and lingo used by those in the vampiric community. You may notice that some of the terms included are the same as what is used in White Wolf's *Vampire: the Masquerade* role-playing game. Some of the terms were in use before White Wolf adopted them to use in the game; and some of the game's terminology has crept into common usage. Please realize that this is not a listing of "Masquerade" terminology, nor is it related in any way to *Vampire: the Masquerade* or White Wolf, nor role-playing at all.

If you are new to the world of real vampires, you will undoubtedly find this book quite informative; it will help you understand many of the terms vampires use – and alleviate much of the confusion newbies face when they first enter the community. Those who have been around longer will also find it useful because it is an attempt to give a measure of standardization to "vampspeak".

I created this document in its original form in 1997. Since then, it has continually been updated to reflect the accuracy of terms and to add new terms. Many have adopted and adapted various versions of this document, subsequently making their own independent revisions, additions and deletions, but the terminology document and copyright belong to me, Sanguinarius. The Second Edition contains over seventy-five new terms not included in the first edition (or on the website), many dealing with psi vampirism and psychic matters of interest and relevance to the vampiric community.

I would like to thank Michelle Belanger, Father Sebastian, and Damien Daville for their input when I lent an early version of my terminology document to COVICA (now defunct) to develop for the vampire community. I would also like to thank Sphynx-Cat, Ravena, Lady CG, Lady Slinky, Irony, Vyrdolak, Anshar, and countless others over the years, for their input, advice and suggestions; the members of #Sanguinarius, my IRC channel (chat room) on dal.net for their input, letting me use them as a sounding board, and for putting up with me as I fine-tuned the wording on many definitions; and members of the Vampire-Discussion, ShadowLore, Les Vampires, and Vampirism Yahoo Groups for their information and input for the terms Wicca and witchcraft, Wiccan and witch.

Finally, if you have an interest in real vampires and the vampiric community, I invite you to visit my site on the Internet at http://www.sanguinarius.org/ . It contains numerous articles, tips and advice for and by real vampires (both blood drinkers and psi vampires), donors, newly awakened or awakening vampires, teen vampires and parents. It also has personal anecdotes from real vampires; a vampire guide; searchable directory of all manner of real vampire, vampiric community, and vampire lifestyle-related sites, groups and resources; a community events calendar; chat room; and more. It's a fairly extensive site, so plan to spend some time there.

A Little About the Author

At the time of this writing, I am a 37-year-old female sanguinarian, or blood vampire. I awakened in my teens, and spent a number of years making a fool of myself, without anyone to guide or teach me, hoping to get people to understand about real vampires when I scarcely understood, myself. I started out with a lot of mistaken beliefs, having nothing to go on but what I saw in movies and read in books; I knew how I was, and what I was, but I wasn't how I thought I should be (I tried, though!). Back then, there were no books *for* real vampires, and only a couple *about* them; mostly concerning those into the lifestyle. I eventually came to terms with myself and my vampirism and decided to take a more honest approach to things. In 1997, I launched my site in order to reach others like me, share what knowledge I had learned, and provide resources and information to those seeking it. Since then, it has steadily grown until it has become the sprawling behemoth it is today (Sarah Winchester would be impressed). In 2007, *Sanguinarius: the Vampire Support Page* celebrated its tenth year.

Hopefully without sounding like I'm tooting my own horn, I have been active in the community and worked extensively to provide support and information; network real vampires; publish a monthly news bulletin which keeps those subscribed abreast of important news, site updates, and community announcements; and foster understanding about real vampires. One of the resources I provide is a longstanding IRC channel (chat room) on dal.net; another is a searchable directory of all manner of real vampire sites on the Internet. I mustn't forget to mention "the VCMB", *the Vampiric Community Message (& Support) Board*, a message forum founded by me which, having undergone various incarnations, has grown enough to warrant its own domain!

I am a cat lover, and have three of my own: Boo, Scooter and Socks; I had Munchkin and Bat, too, but they passed on. I'm a coffee addict, too. I love gothic things, ghosts and graveyards, true stories of hauntings, cryptozoology, forteana, and unexplained mysteries. I also love history (the older, the better), antiques, travelling, museums, and ancient ruins. My favorite magazine is *Archaeology*. And I love playing the computer games *Civilization III* and *IV*. As far as musical interests go, I'm fairly eclectic, and like most anything if it's good, except for rap and hiphop; my favorites are old school Gothic, Reggae, oldies and classical. My favorite TV shows are *Cops*, *Ghost Hunters*, and *Animal Cops/Animal Precinct*. I also like science fiction.

You can find out more about me (and my cats) at my personal site, *Sangi's Corner*, online at http://sangi.sanguinarius.org/. I also have a LiveJournal blog, informally titled *Sanguinarius's Little Corner of Babble*, located on the Internet at http://sanguinarius.livejournal.com/, in which I include everything from vampire community announcements to ranting about annoying family members.

It is my sincere desire that you enjoy this Dictionary of Vampspeak!

Sanguinarius, 2008

~A~

ambient energy:

The non-physical psi energy cast off by living things which is abundantly adrift in the environment. It is one possible source for psi vampires to feed from, especially without having to worry about harming anything or anyone. The amount and quality of ambient energy in a particular location may be dependent upon the overall health of the living things in the area. For example, an area with a lot of drunks and drug addicts will not have the same level or quality of ambient energy as one with lots of enthusiastic, happy people.

ambient feeding:

Feeding from the non-physical psi energy which is abundantly adrift in the environment, generally cast off by a group of people gathered in a particular place. (Compare to "deep feeding" and "surface feeding".)

ankh:

An ansate cross, or looped cross, used in ancient Egypt as the symbol of life. Contrary to popular belief, it doesn't actually stand for immortality as many in the vampire subculture believe. But,

The Dictionary of Vampspeak

because of its associations, it has come to be a popular symbol for vampires, both fictional and real. Many Houses have adopted and adapted the ankh in some form to symbolize their organizations. For instance, the Sanguinarius Ankh is a composite of a drop of blood (the loop), bat wings (the cross bar), and a blade (the stem).

astral plane / astral realm:

A non-physical plane of existence, higher than the physical plane, which is home to a number of noncorporeal entities. It is believed by some that they can visit the astral plane while dreaming or through meditation.

astral vampire:

A non-physical entity with vampiric traits residing in the astral plane. Some vampiric cults worship these beings as "undead gods", although they are in no sense deities.

aura:

The energy field, theorized to be electromagnetic, surrounding and emanating from each living being and many nonliving ones. Though it is not generally visible to the eye, it can be perceived psychically as a multicolored field; the colors are said to reflect the being's state of health, moods and emotions.

autovampirism:

The drinking of one's own blood.

awakening:

The physical and mental changes that occur when someone

awakens to their latent vampire nature. The awakening typically occurs during or shortly after the onset of puberty, but in some individuals may take years to manifest. Those undergoing the awakening, undergo various mental and physical changes. These changes often include an increased sensitivity to light and particularly to sunlight, a growing affinity for night and darkness, having one's circadian rhythm become inverted and switching from a nocturnal to a diurnal sleeping schedule, and experiencing the first symptoms of the thirst. Many experience acute feelings of isolation and alienation during this process, as their changing nature distances them increasingly from their "normal" family and friends. Many seek out organizations or groups to help understand their desires and newfound feelings. (See also "turning".)

~B~

beacon:

A particular feeling or energy signature generated by vampires in general, but latent or potential vampires in particular. The beacon seems to exist to attract other vampires to the potential vampire so that they may instigate the awakening process. (See also "vampdar".)

the beast:

The primal, instinctive, animalistic, bestial nature of a frustrated or desperate vampire, where he or she gets really evil-minded and aggressive and wants to just go berserk, rip people and things apart for the pure "fun" of it, and feed violently. It's destructive and cold, and if you don't control it, then you will be under its control. This is different from just "vamping out" but that is when it's most likely to manifest.

black hole:

1.) Slang term for a person, usually a psi vampire, who is unable to stop feeding or drawing in energy, either due to a lack of knowledge or some sort of injury.

2.) Slang for a psi vampire whose energy needs or feeding capabilities are so high that he or she is constantly feeding or drawing in energy in order to maintain his or her usual functioning level.

black swan:

A term lifestylers use to denote a non-vampyre who is friendly and accepting towards vampyres and often supportive of those in the vampyre scene, but who feels no desire to adopt the lifestyle. (Compare to "white swan".)

The Black Veil:

Also known as the "Thirteen Rules of Community". Composed by Michelle Belanger, Father Todd Sebastian and COVICA, this is a set of 13 common-sense guidelines for the Sanguinarium as well as the vampire community. It deals with such things as responsibility, etiquette, feeding practices, the lifestyle, discretion, etc. The Black Veil has undergone several major revisions since its first incarnation in 1997 in attempts to be made more applicable and palatable to the real vampire community and not just the Sanguinarium; in 2003, it was revised once again and cut down to just seven tenets; in 2007, it was revised once again.

blood:

The red fluid that flows through the veins of animals and humans. It contains vital nutrients, performs a variety of functions within the body, and carries the lifeforce within it.

blood-bars:

Rumored underground vampire havens, which have a members-only and very secretive policy. They are only open to properly initiated (usually through a coven) members of the community, if then. It is said they serve stored blood and/or have willing donors who provide blood over a bar. Certainly if they exist they are only a part a of a local population's cabal.

blood bond:

1.) A strong, sometimes undesired, bond or attraction which can develop in a donor towards the vampire he or she is feeding; this bond can be a mutual thing between both the vampire and his or her donor, but often is felt only by the donor.

2.) A rite, ritual or ceremony marking a commitment to a coven or an individual. It is also a term to reflect a vampiric marriage.

blood doll:

Someone who gives blood in hopes of looking cool and/or who may have erotic desires fulfilled by being fed on.

blood-drinker:

Anyone who drinks blood, regardless of motivation.

blood-fetishist:

Someone who is erotically attracted to the sight, taste or smell of blood; he or she generally has no physical need to consume it, and will usually be happy with small amounts. Blood-fetishism is often accompanied by other sexual fetishes, including sadism and masochism, and the blood is usually taken during sexual or fetish play, as in a bondage or domination situation.

blood junkie:

A derogatory term for someone who experiences the physical need to consume blood; a sanguinarian (see also "the Thirst", "sanguinarian"). Particularly refers to one who has no control over his or her thirst and goes around feeding indiscriminately.

blood rage:

A roleplaying game term that has crept into nominal usage by the vampire community, blood rage is similar to "vamping out", but apparently more severe.

blood rush:

The feelings of euphoria, peace and the rush of energy a sanguine vampire gets after feeding.

blood vamp:

A short form of "blood vampire", or sanguinarian.

bloodletting:

The physical act of cutting or piercing the flesh in order to extract blood. This is commonly used for feeding as well as in bloodplay and fetishism. (See also "bloodplay".)

bloodlust:

For sanguinarians, the need to feed. (See "vamping out".)

bloodplay:

Similar to bloodletting, bloodplay is the act of using blood in sexual or fetish situations. Bloodplay can also refer to the integration of blood and bloodletting in ritual. (See also "bloodletting".)

bloodsharing partner:

A more appealing term for a donor. Some donors dislike being called "donors", as they feel it somehow belittles them or their role in their vampires' lives. (See "donor".)

~C~

cabal:

The far-underground "shadow" community of sanguinarians in a particular geographic location. Few even believe they exist and cabals include the blood-bars and other unknown things. Cabals are very selective as to who even knows who is a member.

castes:

The Kheprian system consists of three castes: Warriors, Priests, and Counselors, each having their own unique attributes and abilities which complement each other when paired. These roles have more to do with a person's energy working abilities and preferences than social hierarchy.

centering:

Any process or ritual which clears the mind and aligns the body with mind and spirit on a temporary basis, which provides the optimum conditions for healing, cleansing or meditation.

chakras:

Centers of spiritual energy located in different areas of the physical body along the spine. There are generally said to be seven major chakras: the crown, forehead (third eye), throat, heart, solar plexus, groin and root. Chakras feed pranic and elemental energies into the subtle body. Each chakra is associated with the functioning of a certain part of the body.

chi:

The Chinese term for life-energy. It is also often referred to as pranic energy or life force. Chi is the life force which flows through our bodies on a spiritual level. Energy vampires and many psi-vamps believe that they can manipulate chi and feed upon it to sate their hungers. It is believed by some that, to a certain extent, sanguinarians (blood vampires) also feed upon chi, for a great deal of this subtle energy is believed to be concentrated into the blood. (Also "qi", "prana", and "pranic energy". Compare to "prana" and "psi".)

clinical vampirism:

A psychological condition, such as Renfield's Syndrome, in which the afflicted person experiences a psychological urge to drink blood. This urge is often satisfied with their own blood, and sufferers of clinical vampirism typically bear slashes from razors and knives up and down their arms from where they have drawn blood from themselves. Particularly sociopathic forms of clinical vampirism drive sufferers to attack and sometimes (although rarely) even kill other people in order to drink their blood.

A related condition is known as SMS, or Self-Mutilation Syndrome. This newly named pathology is becoming alarmingly common in American youths. Sufferers of SMS, often known as "cutters", feel the need to cut into their flesh and watch themselves bleed. Some sufferers of SMS also drink the blood drawn out this way, although this is not standard for the disease. Most sufferers of SMS are redirecting feelings of anger, frustration, inadequacy, or emotional pain onto their bodies. (See "Self-Mutilation Syndrome", and "Renfield's Syndrome".)

construct:

Energy which has been molded into a nonphysical/metaphysical form (such as a psi ball, shield, ward, or even an entity) and encoded with specific instructions in line with the will of it's creator.

Court:

A monthly social event which is much like a "town meeting" for members of the vampiric community in a specific geographic area. Court is usually held once a month at a local tea or coffee house, lounge or haven, and only vampires and those within the community are welcome. This is an opportunity to socialize with others in the community. News and announcements are made, poetry is read, new members, elders, etc., are introduced. Here vampires are generally free to escape mundane society. The host of the court is usually a locally respected Elder who secures a date, time, venue, and promotes the event.

combo:

A vampire who is capable of feeding on blood as well as psi energy. It seems to me that most real vampires are capable of feeding from both, or using blood and psi interchangeably. Ex., "I am a psi/sang combo." (Also, "hybrid".)

coming out (of the coffin):

This means the same thing that it means for gays (except they come out of the closet...). Involves being open or frank with people about being a vampire, drinking blood, feeding upon energy, etc. Those who have come out in this way do not hide their lifestyle at all, not even in their daily lives. Many people in the vampiric community choose to be "in the coffin" and are not public about their lifestyle outside of the community or scene.

coven:

Groups of individual vampires or vampyre lifestylers, usually but not always located within a certain geographic area, who have banded together under a specific theme, set of ideals, traditions, common sigil, havens, membership requirements, hierarchy and/or rites. Covens range in size from as few as three members to as many as hundreds. The organization and purpose of each coven varies from fraternal (House Sahjaza); religious (Church of the Vampire -- not to be confused with the Vampire Church); or familial (Clan of Lilith). Some titles given to leaders of covens include Elder, High Priest, Patriarch, Matriarch, or Coven Master. There are no requirements for forming a coven other than a group of people getting together, choosing a sigil, name and theme.

COVICA:

The now-defunct Council of Elders drawn from many different traditions whose purpose is to help network the community, standardize language and terminology, and encourage cooperation, if not outright unification between the diverse aspects of the Sanguinarium and vampire communities. COVICA stands for Council Of Vampyric International Community Affairs.

cutters:

(See "cutting" and "Self-Mutilation Syndrome".)

cutting:

There can be many reasons for someone to cut themselves and a lot of them are neither related to vampirism or "attention seeking" as most people believe. For people with physical pain or problems with depression, cutting can be a powerful coping mechanism and there is no shame in it. (See also "Self-Mutilation Syndrome".)

~D~

dayside:

A lifestyler term for the mundane part of one's boring, day-to-day existence: working, paying the bills, taking the kids to a soccer game, etc. For lifestylers (unless they are also real vampires), the dayside is actually the whole of their existence except for the fantasy of the "nightside". (Compare to "nightside".)

deep need:

(See "the need".)

deep feeding:

Feeding from the essence, the prana or lifeforce, of a person. This is a very intimate and personal way of feeding, and may cause a strong bond to form between the vampire and his or her donor. (Compare to "ambient feeding" and surface feeding".)

dhampir:

Folklorically, the offspring of a vampire (the undead variety) and a human. If not stillborn, the dhampir was said to have special powers of vampire detection, and would travel from village to village, offering his or her services as a vampire hunter.

In the vampire community, the term has been taken to mean the child of a vampire.

donor:

Someone who gives or shares their blood or life-energy, without obligation. Many donors prefer to offer themselves to just one vampire, but some donors will offer of themselves to entire co-vens, provided their offerings are appreciated and not abused. (See also "source", "supplier".)

dreamwalking:

Similar to astral travel, this is the act of entering someone else's dreams through your own dreaming or meditation, either as a participant in the dream or observer.

~**E**~

Elder:

A prominent member of the vampiric community who is hon-ored and respected for his or her experience, knowledge, willing-ness to help others, accomplishments and devotion. Elders are often those individuals who have helped establish a community, organize groups, or help network the community.

elemental vampire:

A vampire whose preferred energy sources to feed from are natural elements, such as storms, plants, trees, waterfalls, fire, and so forth.

elorath/Scrolls of Elorath:

From House Eclipse: "According to the OSV, this is the great vampiric essence and the vampiric astral spirits, called by the Temple of the Vampire the Undead Gods. This is one of the inner teachings of OSV. Some say this term evolved from the word 'el-or-ath', which is the Atlantian [*sic*] term for a vampiric spirit.

However, this is" -- untrue! In actuality, the word originated back in the days of the original Coven, then operated by Raphael Osiris, and the "Sanguinarium" was still "the Sanguinary", and is an acronym for "Eternal Lord Our Regent Aaron Todd Hoyt". Seriously.

embrace:

A hug. Since turning or awakening someone does not involve any sort of hug, where the vampire wraps his arms around a person, drawing him or her close so he can bite them on the neck to feed or turn them into a vampire (a la Dracula or Christopher Lee), I am **not** going to define it as such, -- regardless of the misusage of the word by others. Embrace does not mean turning, but it is an incredibly romantic word for an event which, in a lot of people's minds, is extremely pseudo-sexual and erotic. (See "turning" and "awakened".)

emotional vampire:

1.) See "psychic vampire", sense 2, and especially "psychological vampirism".

2.) A vampire whose preferred energy source to feed from is emotions; he or she knows the right words and actions to induce the emotion they want to feed on. It can be argued that this is just a manipulative psi vampire.

empathic vampire:

Similar to an emotional vampire, sense 2, the empathic vampire can both experience someone else's emotions and feed from them. (See "emotional vampire", sense 2.)

empathy:

The ability to pick up on someone else's emotions and experience them for oneself. This can be difficult at times because it can be hard at times for an empath to distinguish between his or her own emotions and those of someone else.

energy signature:

The pattern of energy, vibes, or the feeling that is unique to each individual; a person's psi 'fingerprint' identifiable in real life or astrally and oftentimes left behind long after a person has gone. Vampires supposedly have a particular kind of energy signature, and those who can pick up on this can identify them as vampires. An energy sig is different from a presence, though you can feel the presence of someone's energy, too. (See also "beacon".)

energy vampire:

An individual who has a need to feed upon the lifeforce of others. Most energy vampires feed upon chi or pranic energy and avoid drinking blood. Some intermingle energy vampirism with blood-drinking. Also referred to as psi-vampires, most energy vampires exhibit the same characteristics that distinguish other real vampires, including light sensitivity, a nocturnal lifestyle, and periods of the hunger or Thirst. (See also "chi", "hunger", "psychic vampire", "real vampire", "Thirst".)

energy work:

A general term for any gathering or manipulation of energy, either by ritual or psi, to achieve a certain goal.

excommunicated:

Cast out of a coven or the vampiric community as a whole. (See also "invisibles", "sin nomine".)

~**F**~

family:

A term used by many people to describe their coven or House, or their close circle of vampires, donors, and friends. Also, a general term for all members of the vampiric community; members of an online message forum or chat room.

fashion vampire / fashion vamp:

This is not a type of actual vampire. Someone who does not have the vampiric condition, and who just dresses the part. A fashion vampire is only into the aesthetics (fangs, contacts, fashion) and not the philosophy or spirituality of the lifestyle -- think "fashion victim". (See also "wannabe" and "poser".)

feeders:

Another term for sanguinarians which distinguishes them by their need to feed upon blood.

feeding:

The act of consuming blood (or, in the case of psi or energy vampires, pranic energy) from someone (or an animal). (See also the "hunger", the "Thirst", and the "need".)

feeding circle:

A group of donors, usually from three to seven, who feed a specific vampire or coven of vampires.

filter:

A psychic construct designed to act as a firewall against unwanted energy while allowing desired energy to pass through. Often, psi vampires use them to keep negative energy out while still being able to feed on the other energy they take in. Empaths may also find them useful to allow positive or wanted emotions to pass while blocking negative or unwanted ones.

filtering:

The act of using a filter to separate out undesired energy or emotions. (See "filter".)

fruitbat:

Slang, a crazy vampire/vampyre. This can be used either in a pejorative manner or a humorous one.

~G~

Gothic / Goth:

Cultural and historical definitions aside, a style of dress, music and decoration involving black and other dark colors; macabre, depressive, and supernatural imagery and themes; and an interest is "dark" things, such as cemeteries and castles, vampires, ghosts and hauntings, death, madness, and magick. Gothic is an outgrowth of the punk subculture; but whereas "punk" is expressed outwardly by aggression and anger, gothic is expressed inwardly as angst, melancholy, sadness and/or depression. Gothic fashion is typified by black clothing; ankhs, crosses or chains; pale makeup, black lipstick, and dark eyeliner; and distinctively nonconformist hairdos. Gothic, or "Goth" for short, is not a religion, cult or gang; and Goths are generally nonviolent. (See also "vampyre / vampyre lifestyler".)

grazing:

This is a type of lifestyle which is looked down upon by the rest of the vampiric community in which a vampire randomly and without discretion feeds upon unscreened donors or sources typically picked up in nightclubs and Goth bars.

grounding (energy):

Transferring psi energy into an object such as the ground in order to rid oneself of the excess, or undesired, energy.

~**H**~

HLV (human living vampire):

A term used to distinguish a real vampire from that of fiction and folklore. (See also "real vampire".)

haematodipsia:

A strong form of haematophilia.

haematomania:

A strong psychological craving for blood.

haematophilia:

An erotic attraction to the taste, sight (or smell) of blood.

haemosexuality:

(See "blood fetishist".)

haven:

A Vampyre nightclub or other gathering place. Considered hallowed ground, the haven serves as the social hub of a given community, providing a place where all the community can gather and socialize. Often, special functions arranged by the vampiric community in an area are held at the local haven.

House / household:

A group of vampires united under a common theme, set of traditions, philosophy/beliefs, sigil and hierarchy/structure. The purpose of a House or household can range from the merely fraternal, to the spiritual. The number of members in a house or household can be as few as three or number into the hundreds, although I generally think of "household" as having a smaller number and "House" as being the larger counterpart, perhaps consisting of a number of households.

Any group of several or more vampires can get together and form a household or House; there is not a requirement to be "approved" by some official council or board; becoming recognized and accepted by the rest of the community, however, is a matter of time, publicity, reputation of the members, their conduct, etc. Some of the more widely known, established Houses are House Kheperu, House Eclipse, House Sahjaza, House Quinotaur, House

Nekhbet; there are many others, as well.

human:

A term used for the purposes of distinguishing those who are not vampires. At best, this term is misleading because it implies that vampires are not human. (See "mundane".)

the hunger:

The desire to feed, also identified as the Thirst or the need. The hunger is both a psychological and physical sensation. Physically, it manifests as an intense hunger or thirst -- but is not satisfied by food or drink. Psychologically, a vampire in the throes of the hunger feels agitated and empowered at the same time. Pulse, heart rate, blood pressure, and sometimes even body temperature, increase in anticipation of the act of feeding. (See also "feeding", the "Thirst", the "need".)

hunter:

Someone that hunts, stalks, threatens, or does harm (whether it be physical, psychic, psychological, or emotional) to someone because he or she is a vampire, or because the hunter believes them to be so; or which gathers information to report those who are vampires. Buffy the Vampire Slayer and Blade fans are not included in this category; it applies to seriously unbalanced individuals who really are on some sort of holy hate crusade and intend to follow through with violence or action. (See also "slayer".)

hunting:

Actively going out and seeking donors or sources in havens or in public. (Some even go to the mall!) This means bringing them home to feed or to eventually screen them. At one point, this was considered safe, but with the advent of HIV/AIDS, as well as other blood-borne diseases, hunting indiscriminately is considered irresponsible and extremely dangerous; there still must be a period of screening time. Vampires who feed irresponsibly are looked down upon; and are sometimes "excommunicated" by their elders for this offense.

hybrid:

1.) A vampire who is capable of feeding on blood as well as psi energy. It seems to me that most real vampires are capable of feeding from both, or using blood and psi interchangeably, so is the term "hybrid" really necessary, or accurate? (See "combo".)

2.) Someone who identifies as both vampire and otherkin.

~I~

immortal:

Term occasionally used to refer to or describe vampires. Though technically, it means incapable of death or dying, it is used much more loosely in reference to vampires, implying that they are not subject to aging, are impervious to disease and injury, etc., and that they are above and superior to "humans" or "mortals". God is immortal; vampires are not. Further, it has not been incontrovertibly proven to me that vampires do indeed experience a capability of an extended lifespan. Check with me in about 20 to 30 years, and I should be able to tell you something more definite about that...

incubus:

The plural is incubi. A male sexual vampire. (See "sexual vampirism".)

Historically, the term was used to describe a reason for the sexual dreams a person sometimes experiences, and were thought to be caused by a demonic spirit which took the form of a male in order to drain a person of his or her energy and lead the defenseless person into sexual sin while they slept.

invisibles:

Those members of the community who, having been ostracized and stripped of their name, are treated as if they no longer existed. Invisibles have committed some great crime in the eyes of the community, and for this they are no longer allowed to associate themselves with the rest of vampire culture. (See also "excommunicated", and "sin nomine".)

~J~

~K~

~L~

latent vampire:

Someone who is already naturally a vampire, but whose vampiric tendencies have not yet manifested. Apparently, some latent vampires may need to be "turned" or "awakened", while others may have their tendencies "activated" by indeterminate causes. Latent vampires sometimes seem to stand out to other, already established vampires through a phenomenon known as the "Beacon". (See also "awakening", "beacon", "turning".)

leech:

1.) A small, bloodsucking worm;

2.) An incredibly rude and derogatory (well, at least disrespectful...) term to call someone who is a vampire.

lifeforce:

The spiritual energy which animates a being and gives it life. (See "prana" and "chi"; compare to "psi".)

lifestyler:

(See "vampyre lifestyler".)

light feeding:

(See "surface feeding ".)

Lilith:

History's first recorded feminist, she was the first wife of Adam, and created as an equal. When she declined to submit to Adam as his subordinate, he went whining to God, and God cast her out of the Garden of Eden, then created Eve, allegedly from Adam's rib, and therefore supposedly subordinate to him; apparently she was, as he didn't whine for a third wife (but since this is not about Eve, I won't elaborate). Lilith was later demonized by patriarchal societies who felt threatened by female equality; still later, she was deified by others. Not a bad job for a lady, eh?

It is theorized by some that, though entirely as human as

Adam, since Lilith had her own complete set of genes and DNA, she is the progenitrix [female progenitor] of a separate strain of humans, which is nonetheless capable of intermingling with the more common Adam/Eve strain. It is theorized by some that this strain is where vampires come from. If this is so, then it could explain why vampirism seems to run stronger in some family lines, yet appear spontaneously or only sporadically in others.

link (psychic):

A telepathic and empathic connection between two or more people. These are used by psions and psychics for sensing thoughts and feelings; psi vampires can use links to feed through. Psychic links are conduits for energy perception, influencing, and communications. In some instances, one can empathically or telepathically influence someone's thoughts or emotions.

the Long Night:

The name for the festival celebrated on the Winter Solstice. Occurring in mid-December, this night is the longest night of the year, and many households and covens gather together to celebrate this. It is a festival of community where everyone relaxes and socializes. It is also the traditional night to recognize new members of the community or a coven or to perform rites of passage.

~M~

magick (spelled with a k):

The art and science of affecting change in the physical word in conformity with one's will. Magick is neither good nor bad; it is a tool, and it is one's intention which determines whether it is good or evil, white or black. Magick is spelled with a "k" on the end to distinguish it from stage magic. (See also "psionics".)

mentor:

A guide and teacher to a new or inexperienced vampire; the one who helped him or her through the awakening. (See also "sire".)

mindfuck:

When someone with psionic talents who knows how, enters a person's mind and manipulates his or her emotions and thoughts to the psion's advantage, sometimes as far as controlling them. The psion uses the person's own vulnerabilities against him or her, sometimes to the point he or she don't know who/what the psion is anymore; the psion also manipulates the person's energy.

mortal:

A term used for the purposes of distinguishing someone who is not a vampire. This term is, at best, misleading because it implies that vampires are "immortal". (See "mundane".)

mundane:

A term used to distinguish those who are not vampires from those who are. This is, I feel, more accurate that "mortal" or "human", and serves to distinguish those who are merely living normal, mundane lives and unencumbered with the life of a vampire. It is not a disparaging term. (See the article "Why We Use the Term 'Mundane'" online at sanguinarius.org.)

~N~

the need:

The need to feed. When experiencing the hunger, one is said "to be in need." Very strong feelings of the hunger are referred to as "deep need". (See also "feeding", the "hunger", the "Thirst".)

Neovampyre / neovampire:

A person who is not a natural vampire, but who is a student of vampyric/vampiric skills, philosophies and/or magicks; i.e., a person who (for lack of a better word) "converted" to vampyrism.

nightside:

A lifestyler term for the vampiric part of one's existence: going to vampyre clubs, dressing vampirically, "letting it all fang out", etc. For lifestylers (unless they are also real vampires), the nightside is as close as they will get to being vampires; it's an escape from their mundane "daysides". (Compare to "dayside".)

~O~

OVC (online vampire community):

Collectively, all the vampires, vampyres, donors, vampire-friendly people and their friends in all the websites, message forums, email lists and chat rooms on the internet.

of the blood:

A term sometimes used to refer to someone as being a vampire.

Order:

A smaller, distinct group which is affiliated with a larger House. For example, House Quinotaur has the Order of Nekhbet.

Ordo Strigoi Vii (OSV):

Also known as Clan Sabretooth Alpha, the OSV is an international organization of people who embrace strigoi vii ("living vampirism") as a way of life and spirituality, develop Xeper, and practice psi vampirism; they disavow blood drinking and sanguinarians, yet still use blood-oriented terminology and imagery (it's metaphorical for the psi vampire). The organization has a history of controversy in the vampiric community, but they mostly keep to themselves. (See also "Sanguinarium".)

otherkin:

Someone who identifies with something other than his or her human side, such as a particular animal, mythological or fantastical being. He or she takes on the astral form of the animal or being when they are in the astral plane. Often, otherkin have physical attributes, mannerisms or thought-patterns identified with their particular being, such as fae having an elfin appearance, or wolfkin having a pack mentality. Some types of otherkin include therianthropes or therians (were-beings), fae or faeries, dragons, elves, angelics, and so forth. Some consider vampires to be otherkin, while others do not.

~P~

parasite:

A completely insulting and derogatory term to refer to or call a psi-vamp or emotional vampire, implying that they are thieves and have no honor.

phlebotomy:

The surgical puncturing of a vein to withdraw blood.

Porphyria:

An acute medical condition which has been postulated by some scholars to have inspired the vampire myths of the past. Sufferers of porphyria have pale, flaky skin and are very sensitive to sunlight. Their gums often recede excessively, giving their teeth an elongated and possibly fang-like appearance. Porphyria is caused by a deficiency in the enzyme which helps produce heme, a constituent of the blood which helps carry oxygen through the body. Dr. David Dolphin was the first to suggest that porphyria was the inspiration for at least some of the Mediaeval vampire myths, contending that some of the sufferers may have been driven to drinking blood in order to relieve their symptoms. As a result, the condition has come to be known in modern times as "the Vampire Disease". **This appellation is very misleading, however, as porphyria only superficially resembles the vampirism of folklore and there is no supporting evidence to Dr. Dolphin's assertion that porphyria sufferers have been driven to drinking blood by their disease.**

poser:

Someone pretending or claiming to be a vampire who is not, with the intent of deceiving others, by making false claims as to their powers, abilities, lifespan, etc.

prana / pranic energy:

The vital, lifeforce energy which inhabits the body and the universe, and sustains life. (Also "psychic energy", "psi", etc. See "chi" and compare to "psi".)

Anshar explains prana, chi and psi: "My OPINION is that it's all the same energy. Prana is everywhere; we breathe it in and it focuses itself within us in channels (Chi). When we send our thoughts and ideas out into the world, they travel through Prana like sound waves through water (Psi). So, psi would be prana charged with thought; chi is prana made to flow within us in channels; and prana is just everywhere, in everything. When you 'feed', you're tapping into the personal channels of another person. In essence, you're directing the flow of their focused prana (chi) into yourself. Once again, many people will disagree on the smaller points of this; these are MY interpretations. I would say MOST would agree with me, but when you venture into the specifics, you're going to have disagreement."

pranist / pranic vampire:

(See "psychic vampire".)

Primus:

A vampire, almost always an elder, who founded or is the leader of a large family or coven of vampires. The plural is Primi.

psi:

A term commonly used to describe the energy which is found within and surrounding all living things, and what psi vampires feed upon when they surface feed.

However, psi specifically refers to the energy that is created (or just changed) when pranic energy is exposed to thought and emotion. Psi doesn't reside in physical objects other than in residual form, because it requires active thought to flow. It is commonly believed that (so-called) psi and energy vampires feed on this energy, but most actually feed on chi, or life-energy. It is also contained in the blood and is believed by some to be an integral part of the transfer which occurs between a donor and a sanguinarian. (Also "psychic energy". Compare to "chi" and "prana".

psi ball:

An energy construct in the form of a sphere. They are used for enhancing other abilities, amusement, or whatever other creative use a psion invents.

psionics:

The study and practice of paranormal and psychic abilities. It's approach is a little more scientific than that of magick, and includes telepathy, empathy, telekinesis, energy manipulation, and so forth. (See also "magick".)

psychic attack:

Any type of unwelcome paranormal or ethereal intrusion intended to cause harm or disruption to the recipient. Psychic vampire attacks are considered a form of psychic attack, especially when forced upon an unwilling victim. (See also "psychic vampire attack".)

psychic energy:

Another term for psi. (See "psi" and compare to "chi".)

psychic vampire, psi vampire (psi-vamp, for short):

1.) Someone who "drains" life-energy (prana, chi, lifeforce, whatever) rather than blood from others. Psi-vampires may or may not consume blood as a means of extracting pranic energy.

Though the two terms refer to the same being, they do so with different meanings in mind. Some insist on calling psychic vampires "psi-vampires", and insist that "psychic vampire" is incorrect, and then proceed to "prove it" by splitting etymological hairs. I disagree. There is a distinction which needs to be made between the two terms. "Psychic vampires" are called such because they feed psychically, as opposed to physically. However, it could be argued that psi is the auric or life-energy where as "psychic" is actually now thought to be shared thoughtwaves from a collective consciousness. So "psi-vampire" refers to what they feed upon, whereas "psychic vampire" refers to how they feed. Not infrequently, psi-vamps may also experience the Thirst in varying degrees of intensity, and in fact, there are many similarities in condition between the psi-vamps and the sanguinarians, with the main difference being, so far as I can see, the psi-vamps' need to drain pranic energy, and ability to do so.

2.) A psychic vampire, in psychiatric terms, is someone who drains emotional energy without giving anything back, and can make the other person very tired, depressed, emotionally unbalanced, or worse, if too much is drained; an emotional vampire. Katharine Ramsland discusses this in depth in her book, *Piercing the Darkness*, (Harper Prism, 1998), pp. 190-196, referred to as "covert vampire". (See also "psychological vampirism".)

psychic vampire attack:

An uninvited and unwelcome draining of one's vital energy, or chi or pranic energy. A psychic vampire attack occurs when a psi-vampire targets someone and feeds or attempts to feed. This can be done from casual contact, from across a room, or even through dreams. These attacks are not always just for draining; they can also be an attack on the mind itself, causing the target to hear, see, and feel things. Attacks of this nature can range from mild to very severe, sometimes leaving the victim despondent or even physically sick from being drained so. It's debated whether one can become a psychic vampire from repeated severe psi-vampire attacks. In general, though, this seems only to produce a condition known as sympathetic vampirism. (See also "sympathetic vampirism".)

psychological vampirism:

These individuals often have a histrionic or narcissistic personality disorder and they are constantly drawing attention to themselves. They usually create dramatic situations and then demand emotional support from those around them. These individuals are emotional vampires. There is nothing metaphysical or spiritual in their condition, it is a simple psychological disorder. Yet it leaves the victims of these clingy, whiny people emotionally and mentally drained after dealing with them. These individuals are not to be confused with psychic, psi or energy vampires. (See also "psychic vampire", sense 2.)

puppy:

A somewhat derogatory term for one who has developed an undue fascination, obsession or bond with a vampire and follows him or her around, trying to gain the vampire's attention or approval, and fawning over him or her, in a manner not unlike a puppy dog follows his or her master around. (See also "blood bond".)

~Q~

qi:

Another term for "chi". (See "chi".)

~R~

real vampire / real vamp:

Someone who has a condition which includes but is not limited to a physical thirst or driving need for blood (which is non-erotic in nature; and in more significant quantity than is generally required or desired by other blood-drinkers, such as blood fetishists) or psi energy; increased physical and/or psychic sensitivities; sensitivity to light or sunlight and a nocturnal circadian rhythm; amplification and/or alteration of emotional states and feelings, etc.; and perhaps the (unsubstantiated*) potential for an indefinitely extended lifespan (which is not to be confused with "immortality"), although many vampires do maintain a youthful twenty-something look well into their thirties or even forties. It does NOT include the abilities to change shape, fly, command others' wills, heal instantaneously, accomplish superhuman feats of strength or speed, etc.

*Some vampires believe the condition does include the potential for an indefinitely long lifespan, but this belief has not been incontrovertibly proven, to the best of my knowledge.

Renfield's Syndrome:

"Some attention has been given to a condition named 'Renfield's Syndrome' in psychological literature, based on the fly-eating character Renfield in Bram Stoker's Dracula. Renfield's Syndrome is described as having four stages: a trauma or 'critical incident' in childhood in which the patient discovers that the taste and sight of blood is 'exciting' or attractive; 'autovampirism', the drinking of one's own blood (autohemophagia); 'zoophagia', or the consumption of blood from animals; and finally 'true vampirism', in which the patient must have human blood, and may resort to stealing blood from medical facilities, or serial murder." -- Vyrdolak. (Apologies to Vyrdolak, whose site is the only site I could find with any information regarding this.) So far as I know, this is not an officially recognized mental disorder.

rogue:

1.) A vampire or blood-drinker's former donor or source who parts company on hostile terms and causes trouble;

2.) A vampire who can't handle things and becomes violent and/or irresponsible, posing a danger and threat to both him or herself and others.

roleplayer:

1.) Someone who engages in role playing games (RPGs).

2.) This is often used as a derogatory term for those who play *Vampire: The Masquerade* or similar vampire RPGs and/or who pretend to be a vampire in their free time when they are not. RPGers are also associated with posers and other fakes who dress the part and pretend to be something they are not. (See also "poser" and "wannabe".)

ronin:

A vampire who does not conform to an organized House or hierarchical structure. Though taken from the Japanese word for a rogue samurai, it does not have negative connotations in the vampire community. (Compare to "solitary".)

~**S**~

sangomancy:

A form of vampyrecrafte, or vampiric magick, which specifically involves the use of blood in the rituals. (See "vampyrecrafte".)

sanguinarian:

Someone who has a physical thirst, need, craving for blood (which is non-erotic in nature) in more significant quantity than is generally required or desired by other blood-drinkers. Sanguinarians (a word derived from the Latin root *"sanguinarius"*, meaning "bloodthirsty") apparently do not get the benefits from pranic energy, or else they are unable to feed psychically like psi and energy vampires, for whom blood and pranic energy are apparently interchangeable.

the Sanguinarium:

The network of like-minded organizations, events, businesses, websites, individuals, havens (nightclubs) and resources for the greater vampire and vampyre lifestylers communities. Inspired by the "vampire connection" of vampire bars, nightclubs and safehouses founded in Anne Rice's *Vampire Chronicles*, the Sanguinarium serves to bring this vision to life as a real "Vampyre Connection". Many real vampires frown upon the Sanguinarium because of the non-vampiric lifestylers it attracts and the artificial pomp and aristocratic hierarchy it endorses.

Note: The Sanguinarium is not to be confused with Sanguinarius Organization for Real Vampires, which is the author's effort to help real vampires, blood drinkers, and vampiric people.

Sanguine / sanguine / sang vamp(ire):

These are shortened forms of the term "sanguinarian". (See "sanguinarian".)

Sanguinese:

(See "vampspeak".)

sanguivore:

A term that I am seeing more frequently, used to define sanguinarians, but which I feel is inaccurate, as sanguinarians do consume more than just blood. I would strongly recommend using the term to refer to those who consume only blood, and nothing else, as their main source of sustenance. I have not encountered any tangible proof that such individuals do exist, and I feel that this is highly unlikely.

scan / scanning:

A method used to gather information about a targeted person through telepathic means. It can be considered somewhat rude, depending on intent (a scan can range from a light, unobtrusive poke, to being forcefully abrasive, to lingering way too long), and sometimes is perceived as an intrusion or attack. However, a scan on first meeting is often seen as a handshake when done politely, but to just randomly scan someone is rude.

the scene, or vampyre scene:

The "scene" is a general term for the social aspects of the vampire subculture including nightclubs, havens, events, businesses, societies, and even the online part of the subculture. Many vampires and vampyre lifestylers are a part of the vampiric community, but do not go out and socialize. Most of the current scene revolves around the Sanguinarium.

seeker:

Someone who is seeking after vampires, or knowledge of vampires, usually desiring to become one him or herself. Unlike a wannabe, the seeker has a more thoughtful approach to vampirism and is willing to learn all he or she can about the condition before jumping head-first into it.

Self-Mutilation Syndrome (SMS):

A psychological condition which has apparently begun to grow among American youth. Sufferers of SMS, also known as cutters, feel the need to cut into their flesh and watch themselves bleed. Some sufferers of SMS also drink the blood drawn out this way, although this is not standard for the disorder. Most sufferers of SMS are redirecting feelings of anger, frustration, inadequacy, or emotional pain onto their bodies. Some eventually get involved in body art and blood fetishism. (See also "clinical vampirism", "Renfield's Syndrome".)

servitor:

An artificially constructed entity which is programmed to do the will of its creator; a sort of psychic golem. A servitor may be conscious and intelligent. A servitor may be used to drain energy from others, or to protect its creator, or any number of other tasks.

sexual vampirism:

A form of psi-vampirism where feeding is done primarily from sexual energy, or energy generated during sexual activity, with or without the exchange of blood. The feeding can be done intentionally or unconsciously/unintentionally. A common term for female vampires who feed exclusively through sex is "Succubus", a word which originally denoted a Mediaeval demon which was believed to visit the dreams of men and tempt them into sexual misconduct; the male version of the word, although not as widespread, is "Incubus". Sexual vampires are also known as tantric vampires. (See also "incubus", "succubus".)

shield:

A psychic construct, similar to a force field in concept, used to filter out unwanted energy or psychic intrusions. Shields can be layered by one who is skilled in creating them. At the heart of any type of shielding system lies the individual's will and belief that it will work, not just him or her going through the motions. (See also "ward".)

sigil:

The identifying symbol of a house, haven, coven, or individual. The sigil often has ritual or symbolic significance for the individual or members of the household. For example, the Sanguine Ankh represents members of the Sanguinarium.

sin nomine:

Latin for "without name". A vampire who has been stripped of his or her name and recognition within the community for having committed some great crime in the eyes of the community. (See also "excommunicated" and "invisibles".)

sire:

A term from *Vampire: The Masquerade* roleplaying system that has crept into general usage meaning the one who turned (or awakened) someone who is a vampire. (See "mentor".)

slayer:

A loud-mouthed dumbass that makes public and obnoxious claims of killing people who are (or who the slayer thinks are) vampires. Just like hit-men for the mafia, those who may be real vampire hunters or slayers are NOT going to publicly announce what they do, as that's a surefire way to the Big House, or the Happy Hotel. At any rate, they'll get investigated. If they are posers, then they will continue to remain free and flap their lips a lot; if they are real, then the Law will deal with them accordingly.

Whatever the case may be, Sanguinarius urges you to report these individuals to the proper authorities. Maybe being investigated will put a reality check in their miserable lives and cause them to tone down their racist hatespeak. (See also, "hunter".)

Whether they are harming or killing people, or desecrating graves and corpses, or conducting illegal interstate commerce (ex., a site on the net, offering vampire hunting or slaying services in exchange for money or goods) -- even if they have had no takers!, -- they are doing or offering to do illegal things, and should be reported. I believe conducting illegal interstate commerce is a felony--?

It's one thing to be a fan of Buffy, or Blade, or Jack Crow, or whoever, and it's one thing to have a ROLEPLAYING persona of a vampire hunter, but if that's the case, then those who do need to put some sort of indication that this is the case!

solitary:
A vampire who chooses not to be involved with a coven or House, and has little if any interest in interacting within the community. (Compare to "ronin".)

soul sucker:
A derogatory term used by those who think lowly of psi or energy vampires. (See "psychic vampire", "energy vampire".)

source:

Someone from whom a vampire will get blood. This is a neutral term that I prefer to use; I feel that it's more accurate than "donor", as the blood's not always a donation...

strigoi vii:

A term meaning "living vampires" in Romanian folklore, it is used by some to refer to the condition and philosophy of being a vampire. The movers and shakers of the Sanguinarium have appropriated the term for their use in describing their more spiritually oriented path, the Ordo Strigoii Vii.

subs:

Short for "substitutes". The various alternatives to drinking blood, usually used when the vampire can't obtain blood or doesn't have a donor. These can help control or alleviate the thirst for blood, at least for a time. Substitutes can include such diverse things as rare steak, fresh vegetables, vitamin supplements, chocolate syrup, or salad peppers.

subtle body:

The non-physical, energy or spiritual counterpart to the physical body.

succubus:

The plural is succubi. A female sexual vampire. (See "sexual vampirism".)

Historically, the term was used to describe a reason for the sexual dreams a person sometimes experiences, and were thought to be caused by a demonic spirit which took the form of a female in order to drain a person of his or her energy and lead the defenseless person into sexual sin while they slept.

supplier:

Someone from whom a vampire will get blood. This is a neutral term; I feel that it's more accurate than "donor", as the blood's not always a donation...

surface feeding:

Feeding from the psi energy from the outer layers of a particular person's energy field, either by direct physical contact or by being in close proximity to the person. (Compare to "ambient feeding" and "deep feeding".)

sympathetic vampirism:

A condition which sometimes occurs in individuals who have been fed from too frequently. This most often occurs in the donors or sources of energy vampires but can manifest itself among the sources used by sanguinarians as well. In general, the victim's resources become so depleted that he or she has to resort to vampirism him or hersef in order to replenish them. In addition to a need to feed, the sufferer of sympathetic vampirism may manifest symptoms commonly associated with real vampirism, such as heightened sensitivities and sensitivity to sunlight. Often, this condition causes some real vampires to mistakenly assume that their donors, -- or the donors thinking that they, themselves, -- have somehow been turned or awakened. But the condition is hardly permanent. This condition may last for a few weeks, although sometimes it can be drawn out for months or years. The best course of action is for the vampire or vampires who feed from the person to stop completely. Without the constant depletion of resources, the person's system should gradually correct itself over time.

~T~

tantric vampire:

A psi vampire who feed through sexual means or from sexual energy. 'Tantric' is derived from "tantra", a Hindu or Buddhist philosophy of sacred sexuality. Not to be confused with "pranic vampire", which is just another term for a psi vampire. (See "sexual vampirism".)

Tease-the-Vamp:

A cruel "game" that non-vampires, or even other vampires, sometimes play where they tease or taunt a blood vamp with either thoughts of blood, or actual blood, which they have no intentions of giving to the vampire being teased. While it might be amusing to watch the vamp's reactions, this "game" causes misery for the poor vampire, and can result in his or her vamping out or worse, if it's not stopped.

tendril:

A nonphysical appendage which a psychic vampire can extend from their own aura and use to penetrate someone else's aura in order to form a link with the person, most usually to feed; it can also be used to absorb ambient energy. A psychic vampire may have one, several or many tendrils present.

therians / therianthropes:

Therianthropes are generally classified as otherkin; however, they differ from otherkin in that they feel they are reincarnated from real animals, such as cats or wolves (as opposed to mythical creatures such as faeries, elves, or dragons). (See also "otherkin".)

the Thirst:

The craving, need, desire, urge to drink blood, experienced as an intense thirst-sensation and withdrawal-like symptoms -- to say the least. This manifests not unlike an addiction, and is very difficult and annoying to have to deal with. (See also "the Hunger, "the need", "feeding".)

The Thirteen Rules of Community:

(See "The Black Veil".)

to turn:

To make someone into a vampire. This is most likely a misunderstanding or misconception of the awakening process. (See also "awakening", "latent vampire".)

turning:

Another term for becoming a vampire. Some groups believe that ordinary people can be turned into vampires, but this is most likely a misinterpretation of the awakening process. The method for this turning varies from group to group, but generally involves a rite of blood or energy exchange between the vampire and the person to be turned. If someone appears to have been turned, he or she was most likely a latent vampire to begin with. (See also "awakening", "latent vampire".)

twoofing:

An alternate, less blatant, and less cheesy-sounding, term created as an alternative for the phrase "vamping out". (See "vamping out".)

~U~

~V~

vamp-friendly / vampire-friendly:

Sympathetic, tolerant or acceptant of real vampires or vampyres; catering to vampires or vampyres. Both businesses and people can be vamp-friendly.

vampdar (a.k.a. vampire radar):

A humorous play on the word "radar" and inspired by the gays' term, "gaydar", this term is used mostly by vampires who are experienced in meeting other vampires (live and in person) to describe the particular feeling they get. It's not something that can really be described well to others, but if you've experienced it, you'll know. (See also "beacon".)

vamping out:

Experiencing an acute flare-up of the thirst. This also in-

The Dictionary of Vampspeak

volves a change in the person's manner, breathing, pulse rate, thought patterns, etc., as their body gears up to go out and attempt to satisfy the thirst. This is a real thing, not a fantasy thing, and I won't let anyone else who does not really have this as a real occurrence claim it; to do so makes a mockery of those of us who really do have to deal with it! (If they don't have it and they claim it, then I wish it on them; let them have it!).

vampire:

A much-disputed term with many meanings, depending upon whom you're talking to. See also the definitions of "sanguinarian", "blood-drinker", "blood fetishist", "psychic vampire", "vampyre lifestyler", and "vampiric community". Here, it is used to encompass all of the above-listed groups into a general category. Also, here, it is not used to define any of those as some sort of supernatural or superhuman beings or someone who has returned from the dead (excluding being revived by medical procedures), and so forth. Anyone who makes those sorts of claims is lying.

vampire aesthetic:

The art and style associated with the vampire. This includes figures with long, slender limbs and pale or bone-white skin, androgynous beauty, Victorian or Mediaeval styles and themes, trappings of lace and velvet, funerary décor, and overall dark and melancholy themes. Scenes of crypts, abandoned castles, and shadowy landscapes abound in artwork that appeals to the vampire aesthetic. The work of Gothic artist Joe Vargo of Monolith Graphics, which can be found on the Web at monolithgraph-

- 46 -

ics.com, is an excellent example of this.

vampire bait:

A poser or wannabe who is just screaming for a vampire to come after them. (What they get may be an entirely different situation than what they hope for or expect...)

vampiric community / vampire community:

The community of people who identify with or have been identified with the label "vampire". This includes blood-drinkers, psi and energy vampires, and vampyre lifestylers. The community also includes donors and sometimes the friends of vampires. (See "vampire".)

vampling:

A young or child vampire.

vampspeak:

All the language – jargon, slang, doublespeak, plays on words, etc. – used by vampires to be able to communicate with one another, either privately or in public. (Also "Sanguinese".)

vampyre lifestyler / vampyre (spelled with a "y"):

Someone who incorporates fictional vampire imagery and trappings into his or her personal life, often cultivating a "vampyric" physical appearance, including but not limited to a very pale complexion, a wardrobe made up predominantly of dark clothing, a style of dress which is modeled on Victorian or Renaissance fashions, black or blood-red lipstick, sunglasses, fangs, FX contacts, and a generally melancholy or lugubrious air. Lifesty-lers often form alternative extended families and social structures modeled on the "covens" or "clans" of vampire fiction and role-playing games. Many also utilize lingo and terminology taken from vampire fiction and RPGs. Some are real vampires in the sense of craving blood or energy, while others are blood fetishists, and still others are just drawn to the "vampyre aesthetic". This is an outgrowth of, but distinct from, the Gothic subculture. (See also "Gothic / Goth".)

There are some people, however, who use the term "vampyre" merely as an alternative spelling of "vampire", not necessarily in-dicating the vampyre lifestyle.

vampyrecrafte:

In general, this is the magick practiced by vampires or vam-pyre lifestylers. Many of them are pagan and follow the old ways, and the ways of magick are an integral part of their beliefs. Most vampires or vampyre lifestylers practice numerous techniques associated with energy manipulation. Many also practice some form of magick, most oftenly ritual magick or chaos magick. Vampyrecrafte refers to magickal techniques specifically designed by vampires and vampyre lifestylers to take advantage of their unique abilities. Vampyrecrafte often has a dark flavor to it, al-though in general it is more of a balance between dark and light techniques.

~W~

wannabe:

A slang term, a contraction of the words "wants to be". Derogatory term for someone who wants to become a vampire, usually with unrealistic expectations of what it would be like. Most wannabes have a very romanticized vision of vampirism, and they seem to think it would improve their lives somehow or make them more interesting. Many are attracted by a false vision of a vampire's powers. They usually fail to look at the practical side of becoming a vampire, such as necessary changes in lifestyle, finding sources to feed from, and trying to hold a job while balancing one's vampiric nature with daily life.

ward:

A shield placed around an object or a location, rather than a person. SphynxCat explains, "A ward can be used to shield general things; example, setting up a house ward to prevent folks from taking undue interest ('these aren't the droid you're looking for'). A ward can be set against specific things or specific people -- as a shield, rather than a misdirect. It can also be set as an alarm, rather than a shield ('alert me if something crosses this boundary')." (See also "shield".)

white swan:

The Sanguinarium's term for a non-vampyre, who often has close contact with, but who is antagonistic towards, vampyres and the vampyre scene. (Compare to "black swan".)

Wicca:

A nature-based neopagan religion founded by Gerald Gardner in the 1950s. He drew from a wide variety of ancient and traditional pagan and folk practices, beliefs, rituals and traditions to synthesize the modern form of witchcraft. Since then, Wicca has steadily grown in popularity and given rise to several distinct "traditions" (varieties), including Gardnerian, Alexandrian, Diannic, Druidic, and Eclectic.

Wiccans honor the God and Goddess, have a deep reverence for nature, and follow the Wiccan Rede, "If it harms none, do what you will". They have covens (worship groups led by a high priestess and/or priest), practice magick and rituals, and gather during special festivals held at various times throughout the year, including the spring and fall equinoxes and the summer and winter solstices. (See also "witch" and "witchcraft".)

Wiccan:

A practitioner or adherent of Wicca, a nature-based religion. (See "Wicca".)

witch:

A practitioner of witchcraft. It is said, "A Wiccan is a witch, but a witch is not necessarily a Wiccan". Contrary to popular misconception, male witches are not called warlocks, merely male witches. (See also "Wicca" and "witchcraft".)

witchcraft:

A pagan magickal practice involving rituals and spell casting, various forms of divination, belief in and contact with spirits, and a knowledge and use of herbs. It seems that practitioners of witchcraft are not as limited to practicing only "white", or non-harmful, magick as Wiccans are (which is not to imply that they solely practice "black", or harmful, magick). Witchcraft, per se, is not actually a religion, though Wicca is; the practice of witchcraft has been around since Neolithic times, whereas Wicca was founded in the 1950s. (See also "Wicca".)

~X~

~Y~

~ Z~

Notes:

CPSIA information can be obtained at www.ICGtesting.com
Printed in the USA
LVOW01s1811170114

369899LV00030B/1008/P